the
bead
jewelry
maker

the bead jewelry maker

stylish handcrafted jewelry to
make at home

cheryl owen

BARRON'S

First published in the United States and Canada in 2005
by Barron's Educational Series, Inc.

First published in Great Britain in 2005 by
Collins & Brown
The Chrysalis Building
Bramley Road
London W10 6SP

An imprint of **Chrysalis** Books Group plc

All inquiries should be addressed to:
Barron's Educational Series, Inc.
250 Wireless Boulevard
Hauppauge, New York 11788
http://www.barronseduc.com

International Standard Book No.: 0-7641-3192-3

Library of Congress Catalog Card No.: 2004111999

Commissioning editor: Marie Clayton
Project editor: Miranda Sessions
Designer: Adelle Morris
Photographer: Lucinda Symons

Reproduction by Anorax Imaging Ltd, England
Printed and bound by SNP Leefung, China

9 8 7 6 5 4 3 2 1

contents

introduction

Making your very own jewelry is extremely rewarding and lots of fun, with stunning results being achieved quickly and inexpensively. This book contains jewelry for every occasion, from simple everyday items that still look special to extravagant, stylish adornments for a night out, a party, or even a wedding. All of these projects would make delightful gifts, too.

The chapters on equipment and materials provide valuable information on what you need to buy and where

you can buy it, and the techniques chapter gives clear steps to guide you through all the basics in order to make the 30 stunning projects. You can then use the clever hints and tips section to get the most from your beads and revamp their style.

Whether you want to make a simple pair of earrings or a range of matching accessories, this is the book to show you how to get going.

equipment

equipment

There are surprisingly few essential tools needed to make the vast range of jewelry in this book. For comfort and safety, work on a clean, flat surface that is well lit and remember to keep sharp implements and glues out of a child's reach.

You will need to keep a tape measure close at hand when making bracelets and necklaces. As a guide, the average bracelet length is 7 inches (18 cm), but this can vary. A loose choker necklace is 16 inches (40 cm) long, a princess necklace is 18 inches (45 cm) long, and a matinee necklace is 20 to 24 inches (52–63 cm) long. For necklaces longer than this, you may not need a fastener that opens and closes; you can fasten the ends with a square knot and adjust the knot to hide it in a bead.

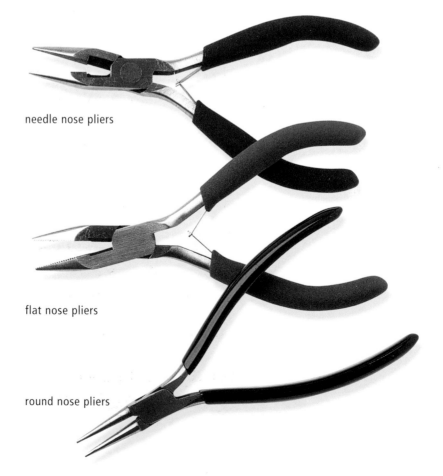

needle nose pliers

flat nose pliers

round nose pliers

tweezers

wire cutters

CUTTING AND MODELING TOOLS

Pliers are vital for most of your jewelry making. If you have only one pair, needle nose pliers are the most versatile as they can form wire loops and press clamshells closed. Round nose pliers are used to create loops in wire, and flat nose pliers will close clamshells.

Ideally, you should use wire cutters to snip wire, although a pair of scissors will suffice for fine wires. Use sharp scissors to cut threads, ribbon, and fabric.

scissors

Pick up tiny beads and findings with tweezers. Tweezers can also be used for holding pieces with one hand while applying glue with the other.

ADHESIVES

Always follow the glue manufacturer's instructions. Super glue (acrylic resin) is strong and will bond lightweight metal, fabric, and some plastics. Handle super glue carefully—it can glue fingers together! A gel super glue is easier to apply than a liquid one when only a small amount is needed. A dab of super glue helps to secure thread knots. Always store the tube upright to prevent clogging.

polyvinyl acetate glue

all-purpose household glue

super glue

masking tape

PVA (polyvinyl acetate) glue is a nontoxic waterproof adhesive that dries clear. Painter's tape can be used to hold smaller pieces in position while you work, or you can use a "stop bead"—thread on a bead with a small hole, and pass the needle and thread back through the "wrong" way to keep the bead still. All-purpose household glue is versatile and will hold fabric and thread.

NEEDLES

Tiny beads should be threaded with a blunt beading needle. Traditionally, these are long and fine. If you find the length difficult to handle, use a short needle instead. Size 10 is the most common; any larger may be too big for many beads, any smaller and the needles could break and bend. Use a size 10 embroidery needle to sew beads to fabric and ribbon. Use a crochet hook to crochet wire with beads.

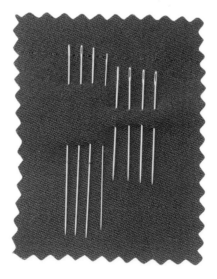

long and short size 10 embroidery needles   crochet hook

findings

Some of the findings used to make your jewelry may be found in sewing stores, but for a more comprehensive range visit a specialty bead store or jewelry-making supplier, many of which have a mail-order service.

The range of findings available can confuse the novice jewelry maker. Here is a guide to some of the findings you will need.

For pierced ears, you should use earring wires. Different earring components in varying materials can be glued to flat pad ear studs

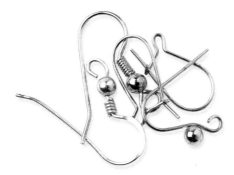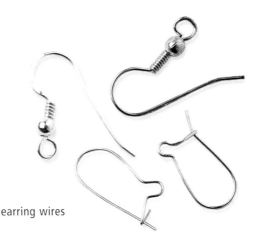

earring wires

flat pad and hung-on ear studs

clip-on earring backs and
perforated discs

or hung-on ear studs, which
usually have a small ball with a
loop to hang your decoration
from. You will need to secure
stud-type earrings to the ear with
a catch or clutch.

For unpierced ears, you can
buy clip-on earring backs, which
can be glued on or covered with
a decorated perforated disc, or
you can use ear clips and ear
screws to hang on decorations.

ear clips

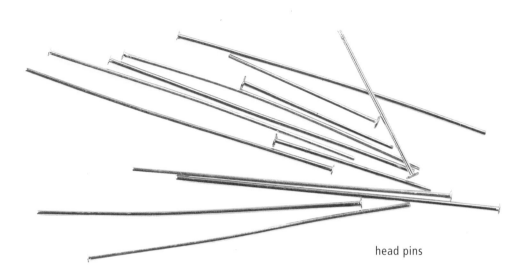

head pins

Head pins (as above) are similar to dressmaker pins but are much larger. They are available in different lengths, although you will probably find that 2¼ inches (5.5 cm) is the most versatile length. Beads are threaded on, and a loop is made at the top of the wire for hanging.

Necklace clasps come in a variety of styles from simple spring ring and barrel clasps to lavish clasps. Spring clasps fasten onto a jump ring, a split ring, or a tag (a flat rectangular metal finding with a drilled hole). You

simple spring ring
clasps

barrel clasp

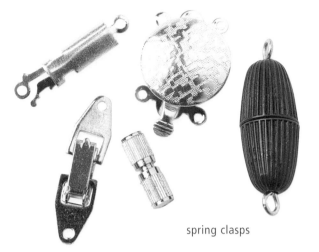

spring clasps

will need to consider the style and size of the beads in your jewelry and choose a suitable fastener. You can attach the threaded beads to the clasps, with clamshell end tips, which are two small hinged cups with a loop attached. The knotted thread or wire ends are enclosed between the cups and the loop is attached to the clasp. End clamps are attached to the end of leather cord or ribbon and then attached to a jump ring and clasp.

end clamps

clamshell end tips

17

jump rings

bell caps

Jump rings join components together and are available in varying sizes. You should choose a jump ring that is suitable for the size and weight of the piece. Jump rings with a diameter of 4 mm are versatile, and have been used for the projects in this book unless stated otherwise.

Pendant holders are also known as bail clips or loops. They have claws that hold your decoration secure, while bell or end caps sit over the knots on necklaces, bracelets, and earrings to hide the less sightly mechanics of the jewelry and to make an attractive finish.

pendant holders

cuff links

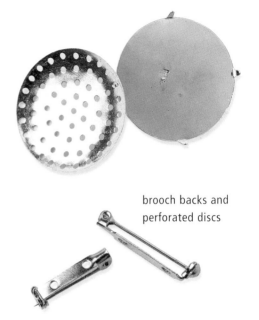

brooch backs and
perforated discs

Other findings you may come
across or wish to use include ring
backs, cuff links, brooch backs,
stick pins, and hair barrettes to
which various materials can be
attached. The perforated discs
you see here can be decorated
and attached to ring backs, cuff
links, and brooch backs.

ring backs

stick pins

materials

beads

Much of the fun of jewelry making is being able to work with the wealth of fantastic beads from all over the world that are now widely available from specialty bead and craft shops.

crystal beads

CRYSTALS AND SPACERS

Glass, ceramic, wood, plastic, and metal are just a few of the materials from which beads are made. The cost of beads varies enormously, but just one or two expensive, special beads on a necklace can be displayed to great effect among small inexpensive beads or spacers. Crystals are particularly effective as they catch the light when worn. Spacers are simply beads positioned between the main beads; they will prevent a necklace from looking too heavy and can add a touch of color or sparkle if they are of a different hue or style than the other beads.

spacers

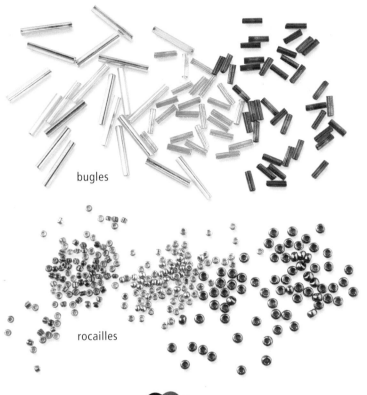

bugles

rocailles

BUGLES AND ROCAILLES

Small glass or plastic rocaille and bugle beads, which are used in embroidery, are available in a huge color range. They feature in many of the projects in this book and can add a funky retro look to a more classic design.

SEQUINS

Sequins are lots of fun to use and inexpensive to buy. They are available loose in a pot or on a string, flat, cupped, shaped, and in many colors. Sequin strings can be sewn to a ribbon choker or cuff, or the sequins can be pulled off the string and used singly.

23

unusual materials

Semiprecious cabochon jewelry stones, or less expensive varieties made of glass or plastic, come in many colors and shapes. Some have holes drilled so that they can be sewn or attached with jewelry findings. Otherwise, you will need to glue undrilled stones in place. Other stones are faceted and catch the light beautifully.

BUTTONS

Always try to be inventive and incorporate unusual materials into your designs. Pretty buttons can be used not only to fasten jewelry but also as decoration, suspended on pendant holders (see the Button Bracelet on page 88) or threaded onto wire.

Buttons have been used in this funky red and pink bracelet project on page 88.

These delicate flower heads have been used to create stunning earrings in the project on page 70.

FLOWER HEADS

The natural world can offer lots of beautiful materials. You can start by gathering flower heads and small leaves to press. Use a special flower press, or press the pieces between sheets of blotting paper weighted in a heavy book. The pressed flowers and leaves can then be sandwiched between pieces of acetate to create earrings and pendants. Drill holes in dried pumpkin and sunflower seeds to make rustic beads, and thread them onto a leather cord among metal beads for a change of texture.

FEATHERS

Craft stores sell feathers in amazing colors for you to use in your designs, or you can simply collect fallen feathers on country walks. To make a simple feather hair pin, tie a leather cord to a hair pin, thread a few beads with large holes, such as pony beads, onto each end of the cord, and slide the beads up the cord. Glue a feather to each end of the cord with super glue, dab a little more glue on the ends, and then slide the beads down to hide the ends of the feathers. Easy!

SHELLS

Shell suppliers and craft stores sell stunning shells from all over the world. Many will have holes already drilled for craft work, but if not you will need to use a fine drill bit to drill the holes into the shells. Remember to support shells on polymer clay when drilling holes.

This stunning choker on page 58 uses mother-of-pearl chips laid on fabric.

MORE IDEAS

A simple idea, especially for children who wish to make jewelry, is to cut drinking straws into pieces to use as spacers between larger beads. For an effective accessory, you can take small silk flowers apart and thread the petals among beads on a bracelet, or you can sew them in clusters to hair barrettes or the perforated discs of clip-on earrings, or even brooches with crystals at their centers.

Small seaside shells make perfect adornments for earrings, as shown in the Shell Stud project on page 70.

LOOKING AFTER YOUR BEADS

Keep beads and other components in containers where they will be free from dust. When working with beads, you should place them in saucers or similar shallow containers where they are easy to select. Before you start, make sure the beads have holes large enough for the thread, wire, or ribbon you wish to thread them onto. If you do not have a bead tray, a good trick is to place beads for a necklace on a towel so that they do not roll away. A white or skin-toned towel is best because a strong color will affect the appearance of your design and the color of the beads you are working with.

A plain towel is perfect to lay beads on while you plan a design.

THREADS, LEATHER CORD, RIBBON, AND CHAIN

Rocaille and bugle beads are light enough to thread onto nylon thread. Large-holed beads such as pony beads can be threaded onto ribbon to add a textural contrast. You can thread ribbon or cord through beads easily by attaching them to head pins or pendant holders and pulling them through. Stiffen ribbon to make a wrist cuff by ironing fusible interfacing onto the wrong side.

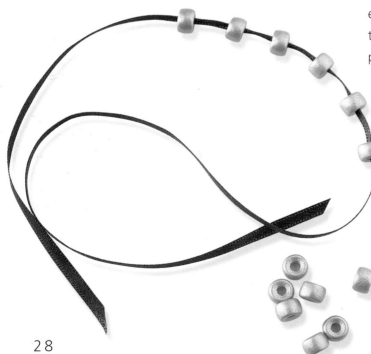

DIFFERENT THREADS

You can stiffen cord ends with nail polish or glue to thread them easily, or you can buy liquid seam sealant for this purpose. Silk threads and specialty embroidery threads are very flexible and will hang well if made into a necklace, but they are not hard wearing and are suited only to lightweight beads. See the Fringed Necklace project on page 98.

USING NYLON LINE

Nylon line is strong, flexible, and transparent. You will need to buy the nonbiodegradable variety to make your necklace durable. It comes in different weights, but generally 20 pounds (940 gr) is a versatile weight to use for necklaces and bracelets. Nylon line is available at jewelry-making suppliers and fishing stores and does not necessarily need a needle to thread it through beads. To quickly make a necklace or bracelet, thread lightweight beads onto elastic thread. Knot the elastic ends together, dab with glue, and adjust the knot to hide it in a bead hole.

This Floating Beads Necklace from page 48 uses nylon line and delicate beads to create a sophisticated piece of jewelry.

29

brass, silver, and
gold-plated wire

colored metallic wire

WIRE

Specialty wire suppliers and
jewelry-making stores sell wire for
making jewelry. The wire can be
bought in various thicknesses and
is available in gold-plate, copper,
brass, gold, surgical steel, and
silver-plated varieties.

The most versatile wire
thickness is 0.5 mm (24 gauge).
A thicker wire such as 1 mm (18
gauge) is suited to heavier beads.

Tiger tail (plastic-coated wire)
is very strong and usually does
not need a needle to thread it
through beads. It is available in a
few thicknesses—12-, 15-, or 24-
gauge—but 24-gauge (0.45 mm)
is a useful thickness for necklaces
and bracelets. Snip tiger tail with
wire snippers or an old pair of
scissors. Very fine wire can be
used for knitting and crocheted
jewelry in which beads are
incorporated in the stitches.

CHAIN

Chain is available by the yard or
meter in different thicknesses.
Cut fine chain with wire snippers.
On thicker chains, use a pair of
pliers to pull a link open and
remove it to shorten a chain.
Beads with large holes can be
threaded onto fine chain, or
attach beads to chain with head
pins or pendant holders.

silver chain

copper chain

gold chain

The pearl and semiprecious stone chain
on page 94 is a perfect project to use
on an existing plain chain that
you own.

31

techniques

techniques

Jewelry making involves using small item such as beads and earring wires, which can be difficult to handle, so there are a few techniques that are very useful to master. Before reading any project, read all the instructions carefully and follow only standard or metric measurements. All the techniques described here have been used throughout the book.

DAISY BEADING

This pretty sequence of beading uses beads in three different colors. Any size round bead is suitable, but the beads must all be the same size. The daisy beading technique works particularly well using rocaille beads.

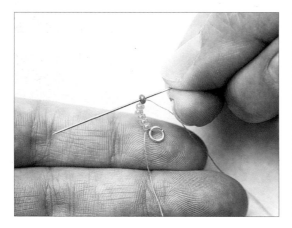

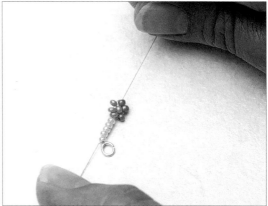

1. Thread a beading needle with a single length of silk thread. Tie the thread to a jump ring, leaving a trailing end of thread about 4 inches (10 cm) long. Thread on five color A beads, four color B beads, and one color C bead. Insert the needle back through the first color B bead toward the jump ring.

2. Thread on two new color B beads and take the needle through the fourth color B bead in the opposite direction. Adjust the beads so the B beads form a circle around the color C bead.

WIRING BEADS WITH FINE WIRE

This technique is fun to experiment with—the beads stand out from the jewelry and the wire can be manipulated to create different shapes. Use lightweight beads; heavy beads such as glass beads will weigh the wire down.

1. To start, thread a rocaille bead onto 0.20-mm wire (32-gauge, as for knitting wire) and adjust it to sit in the center of the wire. Insert both ends of the wire through the hole of a plastic bead, then thread another rocaille bead onto one strand of the wire.

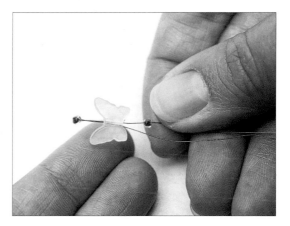

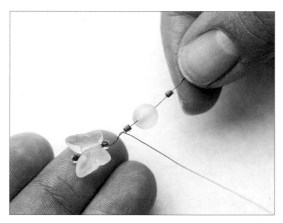

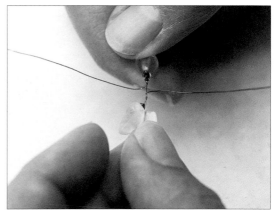

2. Twist the wires together twice after the second rocaille to anchor the beads in place. To add more beads, thread a rocaille bead onto one strand of the wire, positioning it about ¼ inch (5 mm) from the twisted wire. Thread on a plastic bead and another rocaille bead.

3. Insert the wire back through the plastic bead. Twist the wires together at a central point under the first rocaille bead, then splay them open. Twist the wires together about ⅛ inch (4 mm) below the last bead.

ANCHORING BEADS

There are two ways to anchor beads. The first is best suited for creating jewelry that you are designing as you go along. Both are suitable for finer threads or fine wire. If using threads and wire that are thick and therefore harder to manipulate, such as tiger tail, use the second method, as shown in step 2.

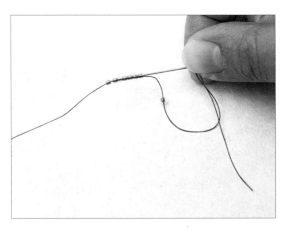

1. Thread beads onto a single length of thread, as shown here, or use fine wire. Insert the needle and thread (or fine wire) back through all beads except the last one.

2. Alternatively, thread a bead onto fine wire, as shown (or a single thread). Insert both ends of the thread through a needle or bring both ends of the wire together. (You will need to use a needle no smaller than size 10). Thread on more beads.

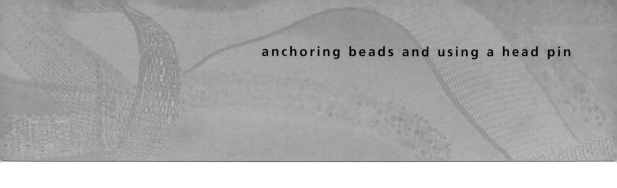

USING A HEAD PIN

This technique is used regularly throughout the book. Beads attached to head
pins can be hung from a chain or earring
wires to create jewelry in an instant.

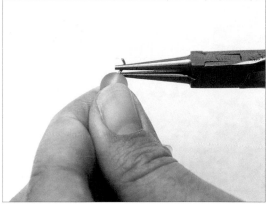

1. Thread the bead or a selection of beads
onto a head pin. Start with a small bead if
the other bead holes are large and prone
to slip off the head of the head pin. Cut
off the excess wire, leaving ³⁄₁₆ inch (6 mm)
above the last bead.

2. With round nose pliers, bend the wire
into a loop toward you as you form it so
that it is centered over the last bead.

ATTACHING BEADS

This technique joins beads together without thread and gives a professional looking finish to your jewelry. A length of beautiful beads attached together will make a simple but stunning necklace.

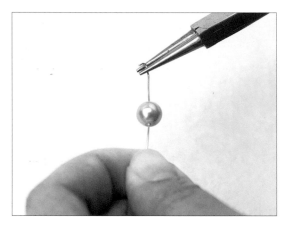 

1. With a single bead or a selection of beads threaded onto wire, use round nose pliers to bend the wire into a loop at one end. With the bead against the loop, cut off the excess wire ³⁄₁₆ inch (6 mm) above the bead.

2. Make another loop above the bead. To attach looped beads together, use round nose pliers to open a loop on one bead, slip it onto the loop of another bead, then reclose the first loop.

ATTACHING A JUMP RING

Jump rings are used frequently in the projects in this book. It is important to open the jump ring sideways using round nose pliers. Do not pull the jump ring open outward because it is prone to snap and difficult to realign. Now slip the jump ring through the hole or loop of the jewelry and close the jump ring.

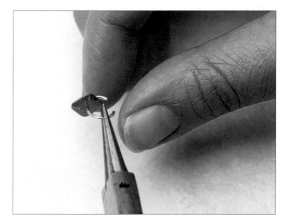

ATTACHING A PENDANT HOLDER

You should consider the direction the pendant will hang—some pendant holders have a loop at the top. A jump ring can always be attached to face the pendant in a different direction or to lengthen the drop of the pendant.

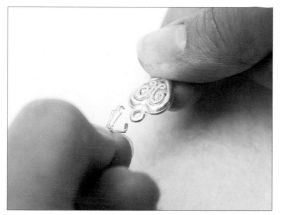

1. A pendant holder that has claws to hold a drop bead can be gently opened outward. Slip the bead onto one claw, then squeeze the pendant holder closed with a pair of flat nose pliers.

2. A triangular pendant holder should be opened sideways with round nose pliers because it may snap if opened outward. Slip a bead onto the open pendant holder, then close it with a pair of flat nose pliers.

ATTACHING END CLAMPS

End clamps give a contemporary look to a jewelry fastener and conceal the raw ends of ribbon or cord. They come in a variety of sizes, although a snug fit is best; an end clamp that is too large will look odd, and the cord may become loose.

1. Choose a size of end clamp that fits onto the end of your ribbon, leather strip, or cord. Dab super glue onto the end of the ribbon, leather strip, or cord and insert it into the end clamp. Let the glue dry before handling the finding again.

2. If the leather strip or cord is a snug fit inside the end clamp, squeeze the end clamp gently with flat nose pliers for extra security. Attach the end clamp to a jump ring, then to a necklace or a bracelet fastener.

MAKING A NECKLACE

If you are making a necklace or bracelet with the same sequence of beads, such as the Daisy Necklace on page 90, one end of the thread or wire can be attached to a jump ring or clamshell end tip and necklace fastener to start, the necklace worked and attached to a jump ring or clamshell end tip, and then to the fastener at the other end. In most instances though, you will start at the middle of the necklace and work outward so you can decide to add or take off beads symmetrically at each end and attach the fastener last.

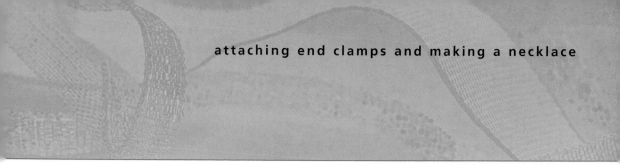

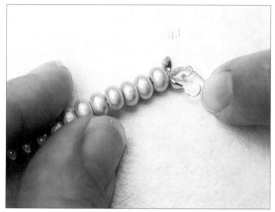

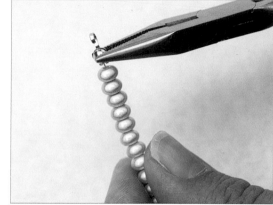

1. Some clamshell end tips have a small hole to insert the thread or wire through. Make a double knot at one end of the necklace. Place the knot in one cup of a clamshell. Cut off the excess thread or snip the wire with wire snippers. A dab of super glue will secure the knot in the cup.

2. Squeeze the cups closed with a pair of flat nose pliers, enclosing the knot. Repeat at the other end of the necklace.

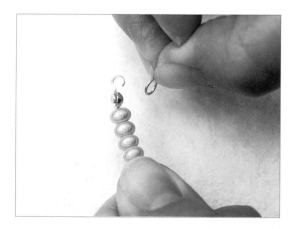

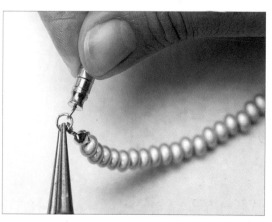

3. Slip a jump ring onto the loop of the clamshell end tip. Repeat at the other end of the necklace.

4. Squeeze the loops closed with a pair of flat nose pliers. Attach the jump rings to a necklace clasp or spring clasp fastener.

ATTACHING A PERFORATED DISC

Beads that are attached to perforated discs have their attachings neatly hidden by a plain disc that is attached to the back with metal claws. You can cover the perforated discs with a piece of fabric in a matching color to your jewelry or, if you prefer, you can leave out the fabric altogether and allow the metal to show through for a more contemporary look to your piece.

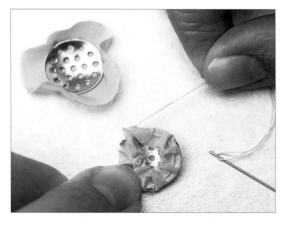

1. Draw around the perforated disc on fabric, add a ¼-inch (5-mm) margin around the circumference, and cut out. Lay the disc centrally face down on the fabric circle. If there are claws on the disc, pierce a hole through the fabric at the claw positions and slip the claws through the holes. (In some cases, the claws will be on the metal backing piece instead.) Gather the raw fabric edges with a needle and thread. Draw up the gathers enclosing the disc and fasten the thread securely.

2. Decorate the disc by sewing on beads with thread or fine wire, fastening the ends securely on the underside of the disc. Attach the disc to the metal backing piece by squeezing the claws closed with a pair of flat nose pliers.

MAKING A BEADED BUTTON LOOP FASTENER

You will need to fasten ribbon chokers and cuffs with a button and beaded loop at the hemmed ends. Alternatively, you can anchor a large bead instead of a button to the ribbon, and anchor the loop around it to secure your jewelry.

1. Thread a needle with a double length of thread. Bring the needle centrally to the right side of the ribbon ¼ inch (5 mm) from one end. Sew on a button with a shank. If the button does not have a shank, thread on a rocaille bead, then the button, threading the needle through one button hole, and then thread on another rocaille bead.

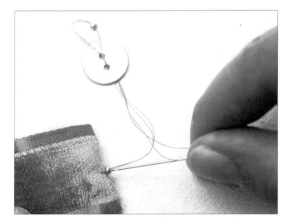

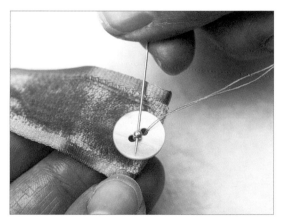

2. Insert the needle back through the other button hole and the first rocaille bead. Repeat to attach the button securely.

3. Fasten the thread to the other end of the ribbon ¼ inch (5 mm) above the lower edge. Thread on enough rocaille beads to loop around the button. Fasten the thread ¼ inch (5 mm) below the choker upper edge. Repeat to attach the loop securely.

projects

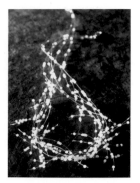

48 floating beads necklace

50 pearl and crystal drop earrings

52 filled organza pendant

54 cascading hair pin

64 dragonfly stick pin

66 rocaille bound bangle

68 colored flower bead and wire necklace

70 shell stud earrings

80 recycled glass bead lariat

82 pressed flower drop earrings

84 loop necklace

86 beaded ring

96 beaded flower brooch

98 fringed necklace

100 shimmery earrings

102 bugle bead bracelet with crystal drops

56 turquoise bracelet

58 mother-of-pearl and pleated ribbon choker

60 coral effect earrings

62 bead and organza necklace

72 choker with silver spacers

74 crocheted bead and wire necklace

76 beaded hair barrette

78 beaded ribbon cuff

88 button bracelet

90 daisy necklace

92 tube ear studs

94 pearl and semi-precious stone chain

104 wire bound necklace

106 fringed clip-on earrings

In the following projects the number and type of bead has been provided where appropriate, but these are only suggestions, and can be changed to suit your own style and taste. You will need to refer to the techniques chapter as indicated for specific instructions.

floating beads
necklace

The tiny beads on this fine necklace appear to float because they are threaded onto transparent nylon line. The front of the necklace is enhanced with extra lengths of nylon line and beads.

Materials

Approximately 100 2-mm frosted glass beads

20 lb (940 gr) Nylon line

2 clamshell end tips

2 jump rings

1 lobster necklace fastener and tag

Super glue

Cut four 21-inch (53-cm) lengths of nylon line. Thread on small frosted glass beads, securing every third or fourth bead to the nylon line about 2 inches (5 cm) apart with a dot of super glue. To do this, dot the glue onto the nylon line, then slide the bead onto the glue. Knot the ends of the nylon lines together and attach into a clamshell end tip (see page 17). Attach the clamshell end tips to a jump ring, and then to a lobster necklace fastener and tag.

Tie five or six 8-inch (20-cm) lengths of nylon line to the separate necklace strands at the front of the necklace. Thread on a few beads, gluing them in position as before. Cut off the excess nylon line.

This unusual effect is very easy to achieve. The necklace can be as simple or flamboyant as you wish. Tie more and longer lengths of nylon line to the front for added effect.

pearl and crystal drop earrings

Traditional crystals and pearls are given a contemporary look on this pair of dramatic earrings. The beads are threaded onto head pins and suspended from hoops threaded with beads.

Materials

Pair of gold-plate 1-inch (2.5-cm) earring hoops

10 4-mm amber crystals

4 4-mm clear crystals

Approximately 180 2-mm cream pearls

6 gold-plate head pins, at least 2¼ inches (5.5 cm) long

Pair of earring wires

Super glue

Thread an amber crystal onto each head pin. For each earring, thread on cream pearls for 1⅝ inches (4 cm) on one head pin and for 1⅜ inches (3.5 cm) on two head pins. Refer to page 37 for instructions on making a loop above the beads on the head pins. Thread cream pearls onto the hoop, and then one clear crystal, one short-beaded head pin, one amber crystal, and the long-beaded head pin. Close the hoop. The beads should fill one-half of the hoop. Adjust the number of pearls if necessary.

Open the hoop again. Now thread on one amber crystal, one short-beaded head pin, one clear crystal, and more cream pearls to fill the hoop. Close the hoop, and dot the closure with super glue to secure. Attach the hoops to earring wires.

The contrast of crystals and pearls always creates striking results. Metal hoop jewelry findings for earrings come in different sizes, and are easy to thread with beads, or to suspend head pins from.

frilled organza pendant

Materials

29½ inches (75 cm) of ⅜-inch (1-cm) wide blue organza ribbon

Approximately 150 2-mm clear rocaille beads

2 ¼-inch (5-mm) blue crystals

1 ¼-inch (5-mm) clear crystal

0.5-mm (24-gauge) silver wire

Clear heart-shaped drop bead

1 pendant holder

Silver thread

Size 10 embroidery needle

2 end clamps

2 jump rings

1 necklace clasp

Super glue

A classic heart hangs from a length of gathered organza ribbon on this beautiful pendant. Crystals enhance the ribbon and suspend the heart.

Thread a size 10 embroidery needle with silver thread. Make a large knot at one end. Work a running stitch along the center of the ribbon with stitches about ¼ inch (5 mm) long, threading on two rocaille beads on one side of the ribbon with each stitch. Gently gather up the ribbon along the thread, making a double stitch every 1 inch (2.5 cm) to secure the gathers in place. The ribbon should end up about 19⅝ inches (50 cm) long. Fasten the end of the thread securely.

Attach a pendant holder to the heart, referring to the instructions on page 39. Thread a blue crystal, a clear crystal, and the other blue crystal onto silver wire.

Glue the ribbon ends inside the end clamps. Attach the end clamps to jump rings and then to a necklace clasp, referring to the techniques on pages 39 and 40.

Organza and silver thread are an unusual and delicate contrast to the pretty crystals on this pendant. You can also shorten the ribbon if you want to create a choker instead.

cascading hair pin

Here is a lovely decoration for the hair. Three strands of exotic beads hang from a hair pin. This is a simple project to create and would make a delightful gift to match the recipient's favorite outfit.

Materials

9 6-mm square red cube beads

Approximately 100 2-mm red and gold rocaille beads

3 3-mm metallic pink beads

2 5-mm red cabochon jewelry stones

1 jump ring

Bobby pin

Beading needle

Nylon thread

Super glue

Refer to step 2 on page 36 for instructions on threading a red rocaille bead onto a single length of nylon thread. Insert both ends of the thread through a needle, and thread on three 6-mm square red cube beads, a 3-mm metallic pink bead, and two or three red rocaille beads.

Now thread on gold rocaille beads until the strand is 4¼ inches (11 cm) long. Tie the strand to a jump ring and insert the needle back through the beads for 1¼ inches (3 cm). Cut off the excess thread close to the strands. Repeat to make two more strands, 3½ inches (9 cm) and 2¾ inches (7 cm) long. Attach to the jump ring as before. Dab super glue on the jump ring to secure the threads in place. Slip the jump ring onto a hair pin. Glue two 5-mm red cabochon jewelry stones to the hair pin.

You can match the hair pin bead colors to an outfit to make it extra special. The cascading beads would also look great hanging from a pair of earrings or a stick pin.

turquoise bracelet

Create a touch of Southwestern style with this attractive bracelet of turquoise chips and tiny bells hanging from a silver cord.

Materials

16 inches (40 cm) of fine silver leather cord

Approximately 9 turquoise chips

Approximately 9 5-mm silver bells

Approximately 10 8-mm jump rings

Approximately 9 head pins

2 silver end clamps

2 4-mm jump rings

1 spring clasp fastener

Thread each turquoise chip onto a head pin and make a loop above the chip (see page 37). Hang each head pin and bell on an 8-mm jump ring. Thread one beaded jump ring onto the cord. Tie the cord in a knot, enclosing the jump ring. Repeat to tie all the beaded jump rings to the cord at ⅝-inch (1.5-cm) intervals.

Check the fit of the bracelet around your wrist. Add more beaded jump rings if needed. Cut off the ends of the cord to fit. Enclose the ends of the cord inside the end clamps (see page 40). Attach the end clamps to 4-mm jump rings, and then to a spring clasp ring fastened to an 8-mm jump ring.

This delightful bracelet is great for everyday wear. The silver strip and tiny bells add just a touch of glamor.

mother-of-pearl and pleated ribbon choker

Narrow knife pleats are worked along the length of this elegant choker. Each pleat is secured with a mother-of-pearl chip held in place with a gold rocaille bead. A mother-of-pearl button and loop of rocaille beads provide a simple fastener at the back.

Materials

¾ yard (70 cm) of ⅝-inch (1.5-cm) wide gold ribbon

Approximately 21 mother-of-pearl chips

Approximately 21 2-mm gold rocaille beads

1 mother-of-pearl button

Matching sewing thread

Size 10 embroidery needle

Starting 1¼ inches (3 cm) from one end, press the ribbon into twenty-one pleats ¼ inch (5 mm) deep and ⅝ inch (1.5 cm) apart. Pin the pleats in place, then check the length around your neck and add more pleats if necessary. Using a size 10 embroidery needle and matching thread, knot a double length of thread. Bring the thread to the right side through the center of one pleat and thread on a mother-of-pearl chip and a gold rocaille bead. Insert the needle back through the chip and fasten the thread on the underside of the choker. Anchor the mother-of-pearl chips to all the pleats with the rocaille beads. Check the fit of the choker and turn under the ends of the ribbon so that they meet end to end. Hand sew the ends in place and make a small hem to ensure that the ends do not unravel.

See page 43 to make the button and loop fastener. To attach the button, bring the needle to the right side of the center of the choker ¼ inch (5 mm) from one end. Thread on a rocaille bead, a mother-of-pearl button, and another rocaille bead. Insert the needle back through the button and the first rocaille bead. Repeat to secure the button. Fasten the thread to the turned under other end of the choker ¼ inch (5 mm) above the lower edge. Thread on enough rocaille beads to loop around the button. Fasten the thread ¼ inch (5 mm) below the upper edge of the choker. Repeat to secure the loop.

The pleats on this choker create a lovely effect, especially when metallic ribbon is used as a contrast to the mother-of-pearl chips.

coral effect earrings

The jagged strands of real coral are recreated here on these beautiful earrings by clever threading, using coral-colored rocaille beads. The beads are threaded onto a single length of thread, and then offshoots of beads are threaded on and anchored in place.

Materials

Approximately 200 2-mm coral-colored rocaille beads

Beading needle

Nylon thread

2 jump rings

Pair of earring wires

Super glue

Thread a needle with a single length of nylon thread. Thread 43 rocaille beads onto the thread for the stem of the coral. Insert the needle back through the second, third, and fourth from last beads to anchor the beads. Thread on four beads and insert the needle back through the second, third, and fourth from last beads. Working toward the start of the stem, insert the needle through six stem beads.

Thread on seven beads. Insert the needle through the second, third, and fourth from last beads. Thread on four beads, then insert the needle through the second, third, and fourth from last beads and work through the three beads leading back to the stem. Working toward the start of the stem, insert the needle through three stem beads. Repeat this process once.

Thread on 10 beads. Insert the needle through the second, third, and fourth from last beads. Thread on four beads, insert the needle through the second, third, and fourth from last beads and then through the six beads leading back to the stem. Working toward the start of the stem, insert the needle through three stem beads.

Repeat the steps in the last two paragraphs three times. Then thread on seven beads. Insert the needle through the second, third, and fourth from last beads. Then thread on four beads, and insert the needle through the second, third, and fourth from last beads and then through the three beads leading back to the stem. Insert the needle through the remaining stem beads.

Thread both threads through the needle. Tie the threads to a jump ring. Insert the needle back through the stem beads for 1 inch (2.5 cm). Cut off the excess thread. Dab the thread on the jump ring with super glue to secure. Repeat to make a matching earring. Hang the jump rings on earring wires.

These stunning earrings show off the anchoring beads technique on page 36 to great effect.

bead and organza necklace

This delicate necklace of fine organza ribbons and clear beads is very simple to put together. Choose beads with holes at least 3 mm in diameter to take the ribbon. Pony beads, which are inexpensive and widely available, are ideal. The pony beads used here are 5-mm beads.

Materials

2 yards (1m, 80 cm) of ¼-inch (5-mm) wide pink organza ribbon

20 0.5-mm plastic beads with large holes, e.g., pony beads

Sewing needle and thread

Large-eyed needle

2 end clamps

2 jump rings

Toggle clasp necklace fastener

Super glue

Cut the ribbon into four lengths measuring 15¾ inches (40 cm), 17 inches (43 cm), 18¼ inches (46 cm), and 19½ inches (49 cm). Sew all the ribbons together at one end with a few stitches using a sewing needle and thread. Slip one extending ribbon end through the large-eyed needle, and thread on five beads. Repeat on the other ribbons.

Secure the other ends of the ribbons together using a sewing needle and thread. Glue the ribbon ends inside the end clamps. Attach the end clamps to jump rings, and then to a toggle clasp necklace fastener, referring to the techniques on pages 39 and 40. Move the beads along the ribbon so that they are sitting in different positions.

The materials for this charming necklace are surprisingly inexpensive. Its dainty appearance makes it ideal as an accessory for a bride or bridesmaid.

dragonfly stick pin

This hovering dragonfly is surprisingly easy to create. Before you start, make sure the holes of the pale blue and turquoise beads are large enough to slip onto the stick pin and that the 5-mm size beads can also be threaded onto the stick pin with four wires running through the beads.

Materials

Silver stick pin

7 4-mm pale blue pearlized beads

3 4-mm turquoise pearlized beads

1 5-mm pale blue pearlized bead

6 5-mm turquoise pearlized beads

Approximately 120 2-mm silver beads

0.20-mm silver wire (32-gauge, as for knitting wire)

Super glue

Thread 114 tiny silver beads onto wire. Insert one end of the wire back through the 57th bead and the other end of the wire through the 58th bead to form a pair of wings with the wire ends extending from the center. Snip the extending wires to 4 inches (10 cm) long. Thread five 5-mm turquoise beads onto the extending wires to form the body.

Thread a tiny silver bead onto an 8-inch (20-cm) length of wire. Adjust the bead to sit in the center of the wire. Insert the wire ends through six 4-mm pale blue beads, and then three 4-mm turquoise beads to form the tail. See step 2 on page 36. Insert the wires through the body beads at the opposite end of the wings.

Thread a 4-mm pale blue bead onto the stick pin. Follow this with a 5-mm pale blue bead and the remaining 5-mm turquoise bead for the head of the dragonfly. Starting at the wing end of the body, insert the stick pin through the body beads. Pull all the wires tight. Dab glue on the wires at each end of the body. Cut off the excess wires.

This elegant dragonfly will look great slipped onto the lapel of a jacket. The tail tip and wings can be curled into different shapes to suit your style.

rocaille bound bangle

Transform an inexpensive, plain plastic bangle into a colorful exhibit by binding it with rocaille beads. Choose coordinating colors such as the pretty reds, pinks, and apricots used here.

Materials

Plastic bangle

Approximately 3000 2-mm red, pink, and apricot rocaille beads

Beading needle

Nylon thread

All-purpose household glue

Thread the needle with a long length of nylon thread, knotting the ends together. Slip the needle through the bangle and insert the needle between the threads. Pull the threads tight so the bangle hangs from the threads. Glue the knot to the bangle. Next, thread on beads, mixing the colors and pushing them along the thread. Wrap the beads around the bangle as you work.

When the thread runs out, cut off the needle and glue the thread ends to the bangle. Fasten a new length to the bangle as before, close to the last bead. Insert the needle through the last four beads and continue threading on beads. When the bangle is covered, insert the needle through the first four beads. Part the first two rows of beads and bind the thread around the bangle a couple of times. Glue in place.

This interesting technique will give new life to a scruffy old bangle. Simply bind the bangle with lots of subtly toned rocaille beads.

colored flower bead and wire necklace

Materials

Approximately 36 8-mm to 1.4 cm pink, lilac flower-, leaf-, and butterfly-shaped plastic beads

Approximately 10 6-mm to 8-mm diameter pink and lilac plastic beads

Approximately 5 4-mm pink and lilac plastic beads

Approximately 12 3-mm purple pearls

Approximately 50 1.5-mm two-tone blue and purple rocaille beads

0.20-mm wire (32-gauge, as for knitting wire)

2 clamshell end tips

2 jump rings

This whimsical necklace is festooned with masses of beautiful flower-, leaf-, and butterfly-shaped beads nestling with tiny colored pearls. The beads are hung on fine wire which can easily be bent into shape.

Cut three 43½-inch (110-cm) lengths of wire. Refer to the Wiring Beads With Fine Wire technique on page 35 to apply two flower-shaped, one butterfly-shaped, and one round bead to the center of one wire. Thread a pearl bead onto one-half of the wire. Twist the wires together twice to secure the beads. Match the beaded center of the first wire to the center of the other wires and twist together twice each side of the center to join the three wires together. Working out from the center, wire beads and pearls to each wire. Add some leaves by threading the wire through their bases, twisting the three wires together occasionally as you work.

When the necklace is 7½ inches (19 cm) long, thread a pearl, a 4-mm bead, and another pearl onto one wire, twisting the three wires together between each one. Double knot the three wires together 3½ inches (9 cm) after the last bead. Repeat at other end of the necklace. Cut off the excess wire. Attach the knots in clamshell end tips, (see page 17). Attach jump rings to the clamshell end tips and then to a necklace clasp.

The finely detailed beads resembling flowers, leaves, and butterflies really make this necklace special. For added interest, select both opaque and transparent beads.

shell stud earrings

The subtle colors of this pair of pretty earrings are inspired by the sea. Select a pair of shells of a similar size. Shells with holes already drilled for jewelry making are sometimes available from craft stores. Alternatively, drill holes yourself using a small drill bit.

Materials

2 drilled shells

6 5-mm white pearls

2 3-mm pale blue crystals

2 3-mm medium blue crystals

2 5-mm deep blue crystals

6 1-mm turquoise rocaille beads

10 1-mm pale pink rocaille beads

2 head pins

0.5-mm (gauge 24) gold-plate wire

2 jump rings

Pair of ear studs

Thread a white pearl, then a pale blue crystal, a turquoise rocaille bead, and five pale pink rocaille beads onto a head pin. On another head pin, thread on a white pearl, a medium blue crystal, and a turquoise bead. Bend the ends of the head pins into loops above the beads (see page 37).

Thread a white pearl, a deep blue crystal, and a turquoise rocaille bead onto wire. Attach one end of the wire to the drilled hole of the shell and the other end onto a jump ring, following the instructions on page 39. Attach the head pins to the lower loop of the attached beads. Attach the jump ring to an ear stud. Repeat to make a matching ear stud.

White pearls and crystals in shades of blue enhance the nautical theme of this pair of ear studs. The beads dangle on head pins caught at the top of the shells.

choker with silver spacers

Create this expensive looking choker using a selection of pretty blue beads and crystals set between metal spacers—bars with holes drilled through for threading wire or thread. The rows of beads are fastened to end bars, which match the spacers but have loops to fasten to jump rings and the clasp.

Materials

Approximately 250 4-mm to 8-mm diameter blue beads and crystals

6 three-hole spacers

2 three-hole end bars

Tiger tail

2 jump rings

1 necklace clasp

Decide upon the finished length you wish the choker to be. Attach jump rings to the end bars and then to a necklace clasp. Measure the width of the end bars with the clasp between them and the width of the six spacers. Take this total measurement off the finished choker length. Divide the new measurement by seven.

Tie a length of tiger tail to the center hole on an end bar, leave a trailing end of tiger tail about 4 inches (10 cm) long. Thread on beads for the length of the final measurement, which has been previously calculated. This will be the first section. Insert the tiger tail through the center hole of a spacer. Repeat to thread on beads for the length of the final measurement until you have seven equal sections of beads with spacers between them. Cut off the tiger tail about 4 inches (10 cm) from the last bead. You may wish to wrap a piece of masking tape around the tiger tail after the last beads to keep them from falling off.

Repeat to make three strands. The sequence of beads can alter, but each section must be the same length. Check that the strands are all the same length and adjust if necessary. Tie the tiger tails to the other end spacer. Thread the trailing ends back through the beads and cut off the excess tiger tail.

Pale blue and silver is always a lovely, fresh color combination, as this choker demonstrates. Follow the instructions to make a matching cuff.

crocheted bead and wire necklace

Avid crocheters and knitters will enjoy making this glorious necklace hung with glittering beads. The beads are threaded onto a long chain crocheted from fine wire.

Materials

Gold-colored 0.20-mm wire (32-gauge, as for knitting wire)

2-mm green rocaille beads

4-mm to 8-mm diameter green beads

Gold bugle beads

2 8-mm jump rings

1 necklace clasp

Thread seven to nine green rocaille beads onto wire followed by one larger green bead or a gold bugle bead. Make a slip loop on the hook at one end of the wire in the same way as you would in knitting. Holding the hook in your right hand and the extending wire in your left hand, twist the hook first under, then over the wire, to make a loop. Draw the hook with the wire on it through the slip loop to form a chain stitch. Repeat to make six stitches. Slide the first bead along the wire and crochet it into the next stitch. Work another stitch and then thread a bead onto the wire for the next stitch. Continue this sequence using a bead every other stitch until the chain is 5 yards (4.5 m) long. Finish off by drawing the wire through the last stitch. Leave a 12-inch (30-cm) trailing length of wire.

Fold the chain into 16½-inch (42-cm) lengths. Secure the folds together at each end of the necklace by tightly wrapping the trailing wire around the end, making a few stitches through the folds. Wrap wire around the folds at the other end, making a few stitches as before to secure. Use the wire to sew a jump ring to each end of the necklace. Attach a necklace clasp to the jump rings.

The knitting wire used to crochet this fabulous necklace is fun to use and shows just how contemporary crochet can look.

beaded hair barrette

There are some excellent imitation suedes and leathers available nowadays, and they are much easier to sew than real skins. This smart hair barrette is made of lilac faux suede with a simple design worked in tiny pearls. The barrette is stiffened with heavyweight interfacing. An air-erasable pen is a felt pen whose ink gradually fades upon contact with the air. It is ideal for drawing beading designs on fabric. Heavyweight interfacing and air-erasable pens are available from sewing stores.

Materials

Approximately 100 2-mm white pearls

5-inch (13-cm) square of lilac faux suede

Size 10 embroidery needle

Matching sewing thread

4- × 2¼-inch (10- × 6-cm) rectangle of heavyweight interfacing

Barrette

Air-erasable pen

All-purpose household glue

Cut a 4¾- × 2¾-inch (12- × 8-cm) rectangle of lilac faux suede. Draw a simple design centrally 1¼ inches (3 cm) within the outer edges using an air-erasable pen. Alternatively, score the design on the faux suede with a needle. Sew tiny white pearls along the design using a single strand of sewing thread, placing the beads ⅟₁₆ inch (1 mm) apart.

Cut a 4- × 2¼-inch (10- × 6-cm) rectangle of heavyweight interfacing. Glue sparingly to the center of the back of the beaded panel. Glue the corners, then the edges of the faux suede to the back of the interfacing. Cut a 3¾- × 2-inch (9.5- × 5.5-cm) rectangle of faux suede and glue centrally to the back of the beaded panel. Sew a barrette centrally to the underside.

This understated beaded panel is an ideal project for a beginner. It is worked on a highly realistic faux suede and attached to a metal barrette.

beaded ribbon cuff

This handsome cuff of subtle olive green ribbon is decorated with sumptuous beads of different shapes, sizes, and textures. The beads are highlighted by a simply embroidered chain stitch worked in gold embroidery thread. The ribbon is stiffened with iron-on interfacing, which is available in sewing stores.

Materials

⅝ yard (50 cm) of 1⅜-inch (3.5-cm) wide olive green ribbon

10- × 1⅜-inch (25- × 3.5-cm) strip of lightweight iron-on interfacing

Approximately 100 3-mm gold beads

Approximately 60 2-mm gold, amber, and red rocaille beads

Approximately 45 3-mm to 1.2-cm diameter gold, amber, and olive green pearls, glass beads, and crystals

Gold embroidery thread

Gold button with a shank back

Matching sewing thread

Size 10 embroidery needle

Cut two lengths of ribbon and one length of iron-on interfacing long enough to go comfortably around your wrist plus ¾ inch (2 cm). Fuse the interfacing to the back of one ribbon by pressing it in place with a hot iron. Press under ⅜ inch (1 cm) at each end of both ribbons.

The beads are applied in rows ¼ inch (5 mm) inside the long edges of the ribbon. Thread a size 10 embroidery needle with a double length of thread and knot the ends together. Starting ¾ inch (2 cm) from one end of the ribbon, bring the needle to the right side ¼ inch (5 mm) below the upper edge. Thread on beads for 1 inch (2.5 cm). Insert the needle back through the ribbon ¼ inch (5 mm) above the lower edge. Work rows of beads interspersed with a few rows of chain stitch worked in gold embroidery thread along the ribbon.

With wrong sides facing, pin the ribbons together. Sew together along the ends. Sew 3-mm gold beads in a row along the long edges through both ribbons.

Sew the button to the unbeaded end of the ribbon. Sew a few beads on either side for decoration. Fasten the thread to the other end of the cuff ⅜ inch (1 cm) above the lower edge. Thread on enough rocaille beads to loop around the button. Fasten the thread ⅜ inch (1 cm) below the upper cuff edge. Repeat to attach the loop securely.

The rich decoration on this beautiful cuff has a medieval feel and incorporates embroidery stitches worked in metallic thread among the beads.

recycled glass bead lariat

A lariat is a single long strand of beads that can be worn in a variety of ways. Fold the lariat in half and pull the ends through the loop, or knot it loosely around your neck. Alternatively, loop the lariat around your neck and let both ends hang free. This lariat uses assorted beads and is a great way to use up odd beads, perhaps from broken jewelry or a few expensive but irresistible beads you have bought.

Materials

Approximately 400 2-mm white pearls

6 2-cm long jade and aquamarine glass tube beads

4-mm to 1-cm white, blue, aquamarine, and amber pearl and glass beads and crystals

Tiger tail

Super glue

Leaving a trailing end 4 inches (10 cm) long, thread a small white pearl, a 4-mm blue bead, a jade glass tube bead, and then another 4-mm blue bead. Continue threading on beads, threading small white pearls singly or in rows between the larger beads and crystals.

To anchor, starting at the second bead, insert the trailing end through the beads and cut off the excess. When the lariat is 57 inches (145 cm) long, thread on a 4-mm blue bead, a jade glass tube bead, another 4-mm blue bead, and a small white pearl. Insert the tiger tail back through the tube bead and previous beads for 2 inches (5 cm). Part the beads close to the end tube beads at each end and dab with super glue to secure.

This simple necklace is very versatile, as it can be worn in so many different ways. It would also look wonderful worn as a belt knotted loosely around the hips.

pressed flower drop earrings

Pressing flowers is not a craft that immediately springs to mind in jewelry making, but flower heads and leaves can be incorporated to great effect to make earrings and pendants. Press flowers in a flower press or improvise and press the flowers between layers of blotting paper slipped between the pages of a heavy book.

Materials

2 pressed flower heads

Clear acetate

32 1-mm pale green metallic rocaille beads

2 5-mm purple pearl beads

Red 0.20-mm wire (32-gauge, as for knitting wire)

Painter's tape

PVA glue

2 jump rings

2 earring wires

Super glue

The pressed flowers on these smart earrings are captured between two layers of acetate and sewn together with fine colored wire. First, glue the pressed flower heads to acetate. Cut out the acetate in a rectangle around the flower heads. Cut out another two rectangles of acetate the same size. Tape the rectangles together temporarily with painter's tape, enclosing the pressed flowers.

Pierce a row of holes around the edges of the rectangles. Starting in the center at the top of the rectangles, lace the edges together with fine red wire and a rocaille bead at each stitch, leaving a 4-inch (10-cm) trailing end of wire to start. Remove the painter's tape as you work.

Insert the ends of the wire up through a purple pearl bead and a jump ring. Thread the wires back through the pearl bead and pull the wire so the bead sits on top of the acetate rectangles. Cut off the excess wire. Dab the wire at the jump rings with super glue to secure. Attach the jump ring to an earring wire.

Choose a pair of pretty pressed flower heads that are similar in shape and size to create these unusual earrings. The flowers are sandwiched between layers of acetate laced together with fine red wire and metallic beads.

loop necklace

This smart necklace has a loop at one end to slip the other end through to secure around your neck. A few gold charms spread along the beads add a quirky touch to the necklace.

Materials

Approximately 180 2-mm gold rocaille beads

Approximately 40 3-mm gold glass beads

Approximately 60 5-mm pale yellow glass cube beads

Approximately 30 8-mm to 1.2-cm diameter pale gold, deep yellow, amber glass, pearlized and crystal beads

3 gold charms

Tiger tail

Super glue

Leaving a trailing end 4 inches (10 cm) long, thread a gold rocaille bead, a 3-mm gold glass bead, an amber bead, a 5-mm pale yellow glass cube bead, a pale gold bead, and another 5-mm pale yellow glass cube bead onto tiger tail. Next, thread on a 3-mm gold glass bead.

To secure, starting at the second bead, insert the end of tiger tail through the beads, make a knot between the beads, and cut off the excess. Continue threading beads in this sequence: six gold rocaille beads, a 3-mm gold glass bead, an 8-mm to 1.2-cm diameter bead, a 5-mm pale yellow glass cube bead, and a 3-mm gold glass bead, until the necklace is 29½ inches (75 cm) long, adding a charm at approximately 8-inch (20-cm) intervals.

Now thread on a 5-mm pale yellow glass cube bead, a 3-mm gold glass bead, then alternate two rocaille beads and two 5-mm pale yellow glass cube beads for 3 inches (7.5 cm). Insert the tiger tail back through the beads from the 29½-inch (75-cm) point for 1¼ inches (3 cm), forming a loop. At the start of the loop, pull the beads slightly apart and dab with super glue on the tiger tail to secure. Repeat at the other end of the necklace. Cut off the excess tiger tail.

Fabulous shades of gold, yellow, and amber really set off this necklace, and the unusual loop fastener is a stylish feature of the design.

beaded ring

This flamboyant ring has small drop beads sewn to a perforated disc. The beads naturally splay out from the center to resemble an exotic flower.

Materials

Ring back with ⅝-inch (1.5-cm) perforated disc

1¼-inch (3-cm) square of fine lilac fabric

Approximately 19 8-mm lilac drop beads

Size 10 embroidery needle

Matching sewing thread

Draw around the perforated disc on fabric, adding a ¼-inch (5-mm) margin around the circumference, and cut out (see page 42). Lay the disc centrally face down on the fabric circle. If there are claws on the disc, pierce a hole through the fabric at the claw positions and slip the claws through the holes. (In some cases, the claws will be on the ring back instead.) Gather the raw fabric edges with a needle and thread. Pull up the gathers, enclosing the disc. Fasten the thread securely.

Secure a double length of thread to the fabric on the wrong side of the disc. Bring the thread to the right side through the center hole and sew on a drop bead. Sew the bead again to secure it. Working outward from the center, sew a drop bead through each hole. Attach the disc to the ring back by squeezing the claws closed (see page 42)

This lovely ring looks professionally crafted but it is very simple to make. The perforated disc that the drop beads are sewn to is attached to a ring back.

button bracelet

This charming bracelet suspends lots of shiny buttons from pendant holders. The main bracelet is strung with pale pink drop beads which form a wide band because they are wider at one end, causing them to sit naturally splayed out from the central thread.

Materials

Approximately 70 6-mm pale pink drop beads

Approximately 6 1.2-cm diameter round red and pink buttons with two-hole centers

Approximately 7 1.2-cm rectangular red buttons with two-hole centers

Beading needle

Nylon thread

Approximately 13 pendant holders

Approximately 15 jump rings

1 spring clasp and 8-mm jump ring fastener

Super glue

Attach a pendant holder to one hole of each button. Next, attach a jump ring to each pendant holder. Thread a needle with a double length of nylon thread and tie to one of the remaining jump rings, leaving about 4 inches (10 cm) trailing. Thread on five drop beads, then insert the needle through the jump ring of a pendant holder on a rectangular button.

Thread on another five drop beads and insert the needle through the jump ring of a pendant holder on a round button. Continue this sequence of threading on five drop beads, a rectangular button, five drop beads, and a round button until the bracelet fits around your wrist. Remember to finish the sequence with five of the drop beads.

Tie the thread to the remaining jump ring after the last bead. Attach the jump rings to a spring clasp and an 8-mm jump ring fastener. Thread the trailing ends of thread through the beads for 1¼ inches (3 cm). Cut off the excess thread. Dab glue on the end jump rings to secure the threads.

Buttons hold a fascination for many crafters and are often collected. What better way to show off some prized examples than on this pretty button bracelet!

daisy necklace

This enchanting floral necklace uses a traditional technique to form a row of sweet daisies.

Materials

Approximately 200 2-mm lilac rocaille beads

Approximately 200 2-mm purple rocaille beads

Approximately 36 2-mm pale pink rocaille beads

Nylon thread

Beading needle

2 jump rings

1 torpedo necklace clasp

Super glue

Refer to the daisy beading technique on page 34 to make a necklace 20½ inches (52 cm) long, using a combination of lilac rocaille beads for color A, purple rocaille beads for color B, and pale pink rocaille beads for color C. This design uses five pale pink rocaille beads between each purple daisy created.

After the last bead, tie the thread to a jump ring, leaving a trailing end of thread about 4 inches (10 cm) long. Thread the trailing ends at each end of the necklace through the last seven beads and cut off the excess thread. Dab the thread tied to the jump rings with super glue. Attach the jump rings to a necklace clasp.

Resembling a sparkling daisy chain, the daisy beading sequence used here is easy to master. Be warned, however, it can become addictive!

tube ear studs

This pair of vibrant earrings uses colored wires to suspend long bugle beads.

Materials
Pair of ear studs
0.5-mm (24-gauge) turquoise wire
10 3.3-cm blue bugle beads
10 1-mm green rocaille beads
10 2-mm gold rocaille beads
2 pendant holders
2 jump rings
Super glue

Snip 10 2-inch (5-cm) lengths of colored wire. Bend one end of each wire into a loop. Thread a green rocaille bead, then a gold rocaille bead onto each wire. Dab super glue onto the end of one wire and insert that end into a bugle bead so that the bead hangs 1½ inches (3.8 cm) below the loop. Dab super glue onto the end of two wires and insert them into bugle beads so that the beads hang 1¼ inches (3 cm) below the loops. Next, dab super glue onto the end of two wires and insert them into bugle beads so that the beads hang 1 inch (2.5 cm) below the loop.

Hang the five wires on a pendant holder with the longest in the center and the lengths decreasing at each side of the first. Attach the pendant holder onto a jump ring, and then onto an ear stud. Repeat for the other ear stud.

Long bugle beads add flair to these colorful drop earrings. They are suspended on colored wires and complimented by modern looking ear studs.

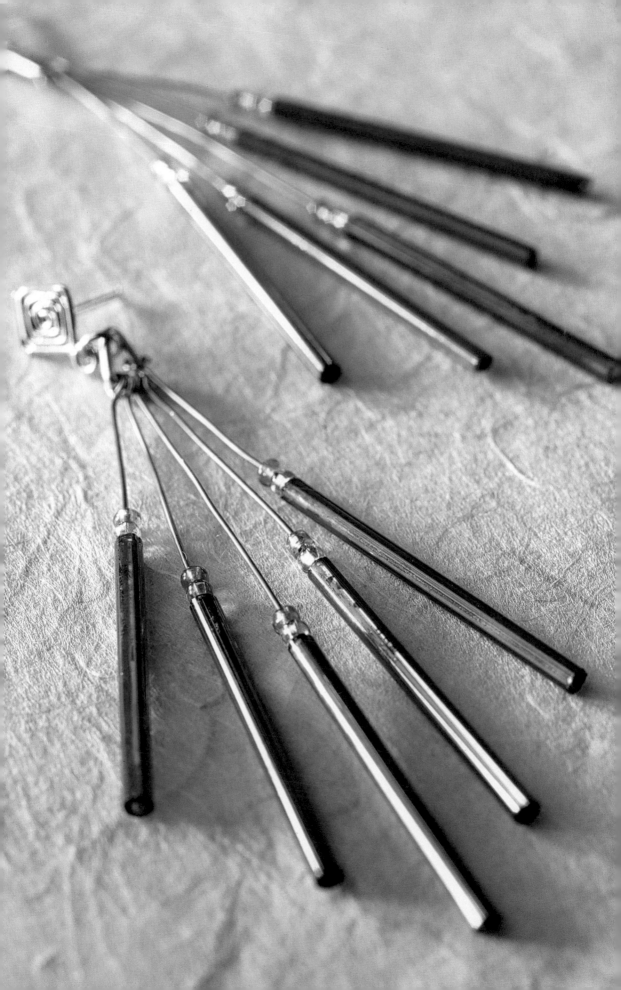

pearl and semi-precious stone chain

Here is an elegant chain suspending lots of glamorous beads in shades of white and aquamarine and highlighted with crystal beads and drops.

Materials

36-cm (14-inch) chain

Approximately 25 5-mm to 8-mm diameter white and aquamarine pearls and pearlized beads and crystals

Aquamarine chips

4 1-cm clear drop beads

Head pins

Pendant holders

2 jump rings

1 barrel necklace clasp

Prepare the beads by attaching them onto head pins either singly or in twos and threes to hang ½ inch (1.2 cm) long (see page 37). When attaching more than one bead to a head pin, choose contrasting beads such as crystals and pearls, or a few aquamarine chips with a pearlized bead. You will need a total of 43 beads on head pins and drop beads attached to pendant holders.

Starting at the center of the chain, attach one bead on a head pin to each chain link. Attach the drop beads to the pendant holders by slipping a pendant holder onto a link and inserting the claws through the hole in the drop bead (see page 39). Attach a jump ring and necklace clasp to the ends of the chain.

This technique is a great way to revamp an existing plain chain necklace. It would also work well on a chain bracelet.

beaded flower brooch

The petals of this dramatic flower brooch are formed from fine wire that can be bent easily into shape. The petals and stamens are sewn through a perforated disc covered with matching fabric.

Materials

Approximately 40 2-mm silver beads

3 5-mm pearlized pale pink beads

Approximately 400 2-mm orange and pale pink rocaille beads

1¼-inch (3-cm) brooch back with perforated disc

2-inch (5-cm) square of matching fabric

Sewing needle

Matching sewing thread

0.20-mm (32-gauge) silver wire (knitting wire)

Draw around the perforated disc on fabric, add a ¼-inch (5-mm) margin around the circumference, and cut out. Lay the disc centrally face down on the fabric circle. If there are claws on the disc, pierce a hole through the fabric at the claw positions and slip the claws through the holes. (In some cases, the claws will be on the brooch back instead.) Gather the raw fabric edges with a needle and thread. Draw up the gathers, enclosing the disc, and fasten the thread securely.

Make a knot at the end of the wire, then bring the wire to the right side through the center hole. Thread on 14 tiny silver beads and a 5-mm pearlized pale pink bead. Thread the wire back through the silver beads to make a stamen. Make two more stamens in the same way.

Bring the wire to the right side through a hole in the inner ring of perforations. Thread on 18 pale pink rocaille beads. Insert the wire through the second hole to form a petal. Repeat to form three petals around the stamens. Work the next ring of perforations in the same way, but threading on 22 pale pink rocaille beads to form six petals. Work the third ring with orange rocaille beads, threading 26 beads to form eight petals. Bring the wire to the right side on the outer ring, and thread on 30 orange rocaille beads. Insert the wire through the third hole.

Repeat to form eight petals.

Use the wire to sew single rocaille beads at any unbeaded holes. Knot the wire under the disc and cut off the excess wire. Attach the disc to the brooch back by squeezing the claws closed (see page 42).

The use of knitting wire allows the beads to be formed into exotic petal shapes on this flamboyant brooch.

fringed necklace

Here is an attractive necklace suitable for casual day wear yet pretty enough for a smart evening function. A selection of pretty beads are tied onto colorful embroidery thread.

Materials

3¾ yards (3m, 40 cm) lime green embroidery thread

Approximately 25 5-mm lime green and dark green glass cube beads

Approximately 8 6-mm iridescent blue beads

Approximately 10 5-mm lime green glass flower shaped beads

Approximately 5 8-mm olive green pearlized beads

Approximately 8 1-cm lime green plastic drop beads

Embroidery needle

2 clamshell end tips

2 jump rings

1 screw necklace clasp

Cut two 31½-inch (80-cm) lengths of green embroidery thread. Knot together at one end. Thread one length of thread through a needle, and thread on about 30 assorted beads. Slip the first bead along the thread to the knot. Knot both threads together ⅝ inch (1.5 cm) from the first knot. Slip the next bead along the thread and continue knotting the threads together, capturing a bead between each knot until the beaded threads are 19⅝ inches (50 cm) long. Cut off the excess threads.

For the fringe, cut three 12-inch (30-cm) lengths of thread. Lay the necklace out flat. Tie the center of one fringe length around the center knot of the necklace. Tie three or four beads onto each hanging end with a double knot about ⅝ inch (1.5 cm) apart. Tie the remaining threads to the knots on each side of the center and tie on beads as before. For shorter fringes, cut two 10-inch (20-cm) lengths of thread. Tie each short fringe to the next knots of the necklace, and tie one bead on each trailing thread end with a double knot. Cut off the excess fringes below the last beads.

Attach the first and last knots of the necklace in a clamshell end tip (see page 17). Attach the clamshell end tips to a jump ring, then to a necklace clasp.

This funky necklace incorporates all sorts of lightweight beads in shades of green. The fringing adds a delightful touch and shows that specialty wires and threads need not always be used to make necklaces.

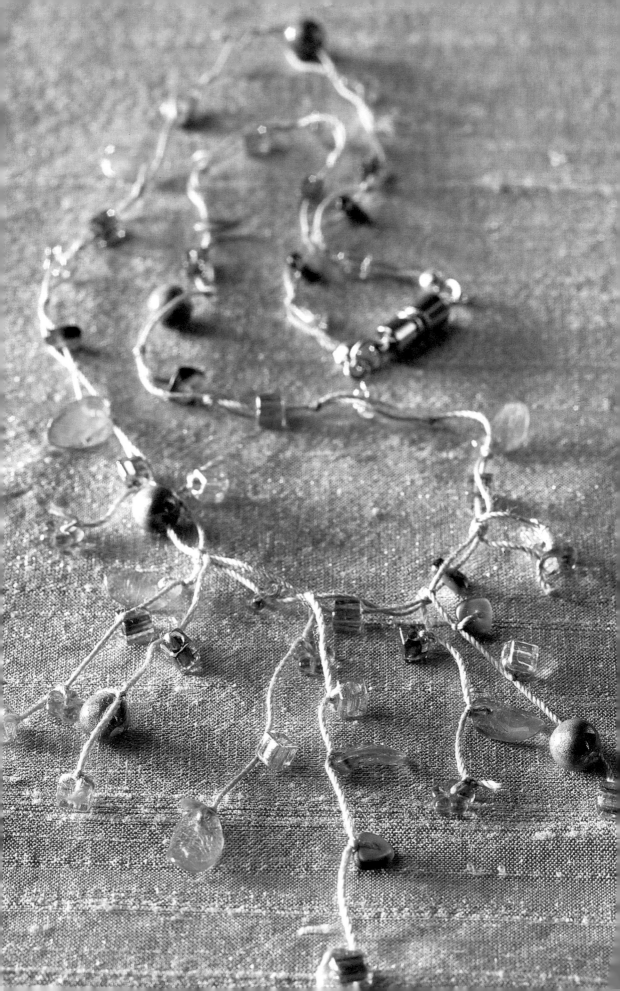

shimmery earrings

Materials

4-inch (10-cm) silver chain

4 8-mm lilac pearl beads

Approximately 20 5-mm to 1-cm diameter pink, turquoise, silver, and blue square and round sequins

4 1-cm diameter clear round drop beads

6 5-mm blue crystals

4 8-mm blue glass beads

2 8-mm purple glass beads

2 1-cm diameter purple round drop beads

2 5-mm clear beads

2 5-mm blue beads

0.5-mm (24-gauge) silver wire

10 head pins

6 6-mm jump rings

2 earring wires

These dramatic dangly earrings are great for a party. Assorted beads and sequins hang from a central chain. Make the chain longer and add more beads for a really flamboyant pair of earrings.

First, snip the chain in half. For each earring, slip a lilac pearl bead onto silver wire. Attach the bead to one end of the chain and an earring wire to the other end (see the technique on page 38). Slip a drop bead and two sequins onto a jump ring. Repeat to make three jump ring decorations for each earring. Slip the remaining glass and pearl beads onto head pins, either singly or with a blue crystal. See page 37 for instructions on making a loop above the beads on the head pins. Attach the jump rings and head pins to every other chain link. Remember to make the earrings symmetrical.

To make these earrings, choose a variety of colored pearls, crystals and glass beads to coordinate with some pretty sequins to hang from silver chains.

bugle bead bracelet with crystal drops

This shimmering bracelet with a cluster of drop beads is simple to make and will compliment a special outfit.

Materials

Approximately 14 7-mm transparent aquamarine bugle beads

Approximately 12 4-mm clear crystals

11 clear 1.2-cm drop beads

Tiger tail

2 clamshell end tips

1 spring clasp fastener and 8-mm jump ring

Thread seven bugle beads onto tiger tail with a crystal between each one. Then, thread on eleven drop beads and seven bugle beads with a crystal between each one as before. Check the fit around your wrist. Add another crystal and bugle bead at each end if necessary.

Knot the tiger tail close to the end beads. Attach to clamshell end tips (see page 17). Attach the clamshell end tips, dabbed with glue, to a spring clasp and jump ring.

The trumpet shape of the drop beads at the center of this pretty bracelet force the beads to sit at different angles, creating a lively three-dimensional effect.

wire bound necklace

This regal necklace is created with white pearls, glass tube beads, and flat gold-plate beads. The tube beads are cleverly wrapped in wire and the necklace is hung with pearls. This project makes use of a lot of jewelry-making techniques and is a good way to try out new skills.

Materials

5 2-cm aquamarine glass tube beads

23 8-mm white pearls

10 8-mm flat gold-plate beads with a loop on each side

20 6-mm white pearls

72 5-mm white pearls

0.5-mm (24-gauge) gold wire

20 head pins

Tiger tail

2 clamshell end tips

1 necklace clasp and 2 jump rings

Thread wire through a glass tube bead, leaving ³⁄₁₆ inch (6 mm) of wire at one end. Bend this end into a loop. Wrap the other end of the wire around the bead twice. Insert the wire through the bead at the looped end. Cut off the extending wire ³⁄₁₆ inch (6 mm) above the bead and form into a loop. Repeat on all the glass tube beads. Attach a flat gold-plate bead onto each loop of the glass tube beads.

Attach five 8-mm white pearls on to wire, referring to the technique on page 38. Attach the pinned pearls between the loops of the flat gold-plate beads. Tie tiger tail to an outer loop of one of the flat gold-plate beads, leaving a 4-inch (10-cm) trailing end. Thread 26 5-mm white pearls onto the tiger tail. Knot the tiger tail after the last pearl and attach in a clamshell end tip (see page 17). Repeat on the outer loop of the flat gold-plate bead at the other end of the length of beads. Attach a jump ring to each clamshell end tip. Attach a necklace clasp to the jump rings.

Thread a 5-mm white pearl and then a 6-mm white pearl onto 20 head pins. Thread an 8-mm white pearl onto only 18 of the head pins. Make a loop after the last pearls, referring to the technique on page 37. Attach the two remaining short beaded head pins to the last loops of the flat gold-plate beads. Attach the other beaded head pins to the other loops of the flat gold-plate beads.

The long glass beads between the pearls on this elegant necklace have been bound with golden wire.

fringed clip-on earrings

These quirky ear clips are fun to make and wear. A fringe of beads is sewn to perforated discs, which are attached to the ear clips. Matching fabric covers the perforated discs to disguise the metal.

Materials

Pair of ⅝-inch (1.5-cm) ear clips with perforated discs

2½-inch (6-cm) square of fine smoky blue fabric

Approximately 500 2-mm smoky blue beads

Size 10 embroidery needle

Matching sewing thread

Draw around the perforated discs on fabric, adding a ¼-inch (5-mm) margin around the circumference, and cut out (see page 42). Lay the discs centrally face down on the fabric circles. If there are claws on the discs, pierce a hole through the fabric at the claw positions and slip the claws through the holes. (In some cases, the claws will be on the ear clips instead.) Gather the raw fabric edges with a needle and thread. Draw up the gathers, enclosing the disc, and fasten the thread securely.

Secure a double length of thread to the fabric on the wrong side of the disc. Depending upon the design of the perforated disc, it will probably have nineteen holes, radiating out from a hole in the center. Bring the thread to the right side through one of the holes close to the lower edge. Thread on eighteen beads and push them down the thread to rest against the disc. Insert the needle back through all the beads except the last to anchor them (see step 1 on page 36).

Repeat to attach beads to seven holes close to the lower edge. Attach beads to the five holes across the center of the disc, making the fringes 15 beads long. Attach beads to the remaining holes at the top of the disc, making the fringes 12 beads long. Sew a row of beads around the disc circumference. Attach the disc to the ear clip by squeezing the claws closed (see page 42).

The matte finish of these smoky blue beads gives the fringes an interesting texture. A very different look can be created by using metallic or shiny beads.

hints and tips

decorating beads

It is great fun to embellish plain beads for jewelry making. The results are achieved quickly yet look professional and costly. Here are some simple, effective ways to make your beads look even more beautiful, all using readily available materials.

Insert a toothpick into each bead to be decorated, then push the stick into a piece of polymer clay or styrofoam. This allows you to embellish it while it is supported, or you can hold the toothpick while you work on the bead, and then stick it into the clay to dry. For beads with large holes use cotton swabs instead of toothpicks.

A quick and effective decorating technique is to apply acrylic paint to beads in simple designs such as spots or stripes. Acrylic paint is available in plastic tubes that have

Use acrylic paint to create patterns.

nozzles to squeeze the paint through, and it comes in lots of colors, including many with pearlized and glitter effects. For further decoration, sprinkle rocaille beads with sequin dust (which is the tiny holes punched out of sequins) onto the painted surface.

Coil pretty yarns around plain, inexpensive beads to give them texture and change the color. Spread PVA glue on the bead. Starting at one hole, coil the yarn tightly around the bead. Cut off the excess yarn when the glue

Glitter relief paint can be dotted onto beads.

has dried. For an elaborate version of this technique, thread rocaille beads onto thread and coil it around the main bead to make beads to match the Rocaille Bound Bangle on page 66. Follow the Rocaille Bound Bangle technique to wrap metal or wooden curtain rings with beads; the screw eye on the rings makes them ready to hang from earring wires.

Paint designs on wooden beads with acrylic paints using a fine artist's paintbrush. When dry, seal the design with a few coats

Acrylic paint is easy to apply.

of varnish. Oil-based polyurethane varnish is hard wearing but will yellow with age. Water-based varnish will not yellow, but it is not as durable. Varnishes are available in gloss, satin, and matte finishes. Gloss is the most hard wearing.

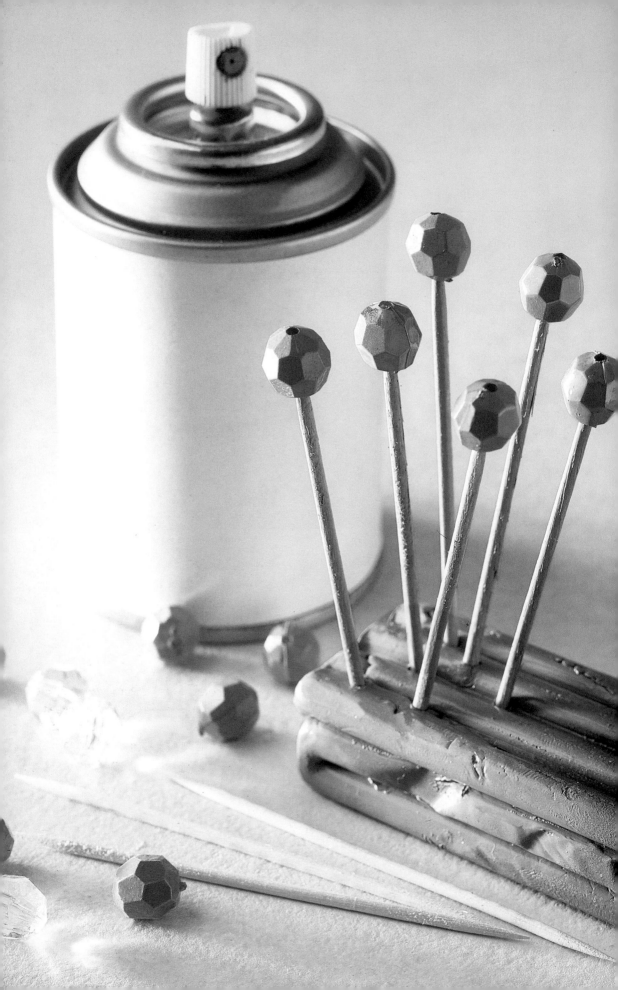

Heart shaped beads wrapped with wire (this technique is described on page 120).

Change the color of the entire bead with paint. The larger the bead, the more effective the process, as paint can clog the holes of tiny beads such as rocailles. Spray paint gives an even finish and is less time consuming than painting each bead separately. As described above, insert a toothpick into each bead and support it in a piece of polymer clay. If you want to reuse the clay, wrap it in plastic wrap or a plastic bag to protect it from the paint. Do not pack the beads too closely together or some areas of the beads may be missed when spraying. Sit the clay on sheets of old newspaper and protect the surrounding area with more paper because paint particles will spread a long way.

Beads can also be painted with nail polish, which gives an attractive enamel-like finish. Some of the buttons on the Button Bracelet on page 88 were painted with red nail polish to coordinate with the other colorful buttons.

Plain beads can be coiled with colored cord (this method is described on page 110).

Slip beads onto cocktail sticks for easy handling, and insert the sticks into a piece of modeling clay to spray paint the beads with a new color.

recycling beads

Being inventive also means looking at new ways to use old and disused materials. Jewelry boxes and inherited pieces can offer a treasure trove of gems, glass beads, and costume jewelry that you may have passed over. These can all be recycled and revamped to create modern earrings, chokers, and pendants.

Save old and broken jewelry. It can be taken apart and the beads given a new lease on life. The Recycled Glass Bead Lariat on page 80 uses old beads in a random way where only a few beads of one particular type are needed. Attach odd beads on head pins and charms on pendant holders, and attach to a chain to

Slip beads from a broken necklace onto head pins to create a smart new pair of earrings. If there is enough left over to make a matching bracelet, you can thread the beads onto elastic thread and knot the ends.

make a quirky bracelet. Of course, beads need not be recycled just from old jewelry. Beaded lampshades, clothes, and handbags are also a rich source of materials.

If some of the beads of an old necklace are lost or damaged, reuse the good ones to make a bracelet or earrings.

Small lightweight beads can be threaded onto elastic thread and the ends knotted for a simple bracelet or necklace. Hang a single beautiful bead on a chain or from a velvet ribbon choker. Update an old-fashioned bead or pendant by hanging it on a bright length of cord for a contemporary look. Thread beads onto hat pins, securing the last bead in place

with a dab of super glue, to create dramatic stick pins to wear in a lapel. Replace lost jewelry stones with cabochon stones in bright, modern colors; open the claws of the jewelry with a pair of round nose pliers, insert the new stone, and close the claws over it.

An elaborate traditional necklace clasp can become a focal point instead of being hidden at the back of the neck by attaching it in prime position at the front of a necklace or choker. Gather together odd charms, tiny keys, fragments of chain, and small defunct watch faces to glue as a collage to a brooch back.

Wrap scratched and scruffy bangles with ribbons, sequin

The hanging decorations on this elaborate brooch can be taken apart to create new jewelry. See the pendant on the opposite page.

116

strings, or strips of fabric. Glue the ends to the bangle with all-purpose household glue. Spray paint narrow bangles in metallic colors, and glue on cabochon jewelry stones or suspend beads or buttons on head pins.

Lightly sand the surface of wooden and metal badges. Paint the metal with metal primer, then paint designs on the badges, which can be highlighted with acrylic paints and cabochon jewelry stones. Use acrylic paints on wood and metal paints on metal. Varnish the badges for extra protection.

The traditional pendant is updated when hung on a colorful strip of leather.

This elegant necklace clasp becomes a dramatic decoration when attached to the front of a velvet choker.

making beads from clay

Take jewelry making a stage further and create the beads, too. If you enjoy other crafts such as modeling clay or papier-mâché, you can use these skills to make some fantastic beads.

Natural and terracotta air-drying clay is available from art stores. Both can be painted but have a rustic charm in their natural state. Polymer clay comes in lots of colors, some of which have glitter added. The colors can be partly blended together to achieve a marbled effect.

Roll balls of clay for beads. Make a hole through the center with a toothpick. Gently reshape the beads between your fingers. Incise the surface with plastic tools or a thick needle. Alternatively, emboss designs with metal jewelry charms or buttons. Or, roll the clay out flat 5/32 inch (4 mm) thick and cut out shapes to use as pendants; remember to pierce a hole for

hanging. Fragments of broken china or mirror can be embedded in clay pendants. Push the clay well over the edges of the china and mirror to secure them. Rub metallic powder onto polymer clay pieces before baking to give a rich metallic finish.

Set air-drying clay beads aside to dry out at room temperature. Bake polymer clay beads in a domestic oven following the manufacturer's instructions. Incised or embossed clay beads can be further enhanced by rubbing metallic wax onto the surface with a soft cloth. The colored wax will emphasize the pattern on the bead. Varnish the waxed beads.

Mix the colored clay to create a marbled effect, or incise a pattern on the surface and rub the baked beads with metallic wax.

making jewelry from wire

Wire can be used not only as a piece of equipment but as the main material in a range of modern pieces.

You can coil wire in spirals and swirls to make funky pendants. Use a pair of round nose pliers to start to tightly coil colored 1-mm thick wire in a spiral. Continue coiling the wire with your fingers. Use the pliers again to bend a loop for hanging at the top. Alternatively, instead of adding a loop, snip the wire about 1½ inches (4 cm) above the spiral. Next, start to coil the end of the wire as before until you reach the spiral to form an "S" shape. Slip a jump ring onto the top outer wire. Colored plastic-coated electrical wire would also be effective for this technique.

Bind beads with wire to add texture and perhaps introduce another color. Thread wire through a bead, leaving ³⁄₁₆ inch (6 mm) of wire at one end; the larger the bead, the easier the technique. Bend this end into a loop. Wrap the other end of the wire around the bead a few times. Insert the wire through the bead at the looped end. Cut off the extending wire ³⁄₁₆ inch (6 mm) above the bead and form a loop.

Coil large rings of wire for hoops. Leave this wire plain, or thread on beads or sequins and form a hook at one end and a loop at the other with a pair of round nose pliers. Hang on earring wires and link the hooks and loops together.

These stylish earrings have colored wire coiled in "s" shapes.

There is a huge choice of colorful wires available in many different thicknesses.

some more hints and tips

- Ideally, light your work area with a daylight light bulb; it is the closest to natural light.

- To stop beads falling off the end of a length of thread or wire while you are stringing them, fold a piece of painter's tape temporarily around the starting end or use a bead stop.

- Large beads will hang in a natural curve if the thread is knotted between each bead.

- Secure thread knots with a dab of super glue or clear nail polish.

- Store wire and tiger tail in coils. It is almost impossible to remove the kinks if the wire is creased.

- Use chips of semiprecious stones; they are inexpensive compared to larger stones.

- Some semiprecious beads, such as turquoise, opal, and rose quartz, are prone to fading, so wrap them in acid-free tissue paper and keep them away from light and heat.

- If you do not have a pair of wire cutters, do not be tempted to use a pair of sharp new scissors to cut metal; it will blunt the blades. An old pair will do the job.

- Make vibrantly colored jump rings from wire by coiling colored wire with a pair of round nose pliers.

- There will inevitably be spillages of beads. Insert a toothpick into a ball of plastic putty and use it to pick up small beads on its tacky surface.

suppliers

All Season Trading Company
888 Brannan, #1160
San Francisco, CA 94103
Tel: (415) 864-3308
http://www.allseason.com
(for semiprecious beads, and
fresh water pearl beads)

Bourget Jewelry Craft Supply
1636 11th Street
Santa Monica, CA 90404
Tel: (310) 450-6556
http://www.ebourget.com
(for beads, bead stringing supplies, bead
cords, and tools)

Fire Mountain Gems and Beads
One Fire Mountain Way
Grants Pass, OR 97526-2373
Tel: (800) 355-2137
http://www.firemountaingems.com
(for glass and crystal beads)

Beadworks
602 South 2nd Street
Philadelphia, PA 19147
Tel: (215) 413-2323
http://www.beadworksphiladelphia.com
(for bead and jewelry designing supplies)

Jerry Smith, Beads & JSBeads.com
120 Windsor Cresent Street
Winter Springs, FL 32708
Tel: (407) 327-4363
http://www.jsbeads.com
(for gemstone chips and crystal beads)

SilverSource.com
2118 Wilshire Blvd. #1155
Santa Monica, CA 90403-5784
Tel: (888) 925-RING (7464)
http://www.silversource.com
(for large range of silver chains, earrings,
necklaces, and bracelets, all available at
wholesale)

WigJig Beads and Jewelry Making
P.O. Box 5124
Gaithersburg, MD 20882
Tel: (800) 579-WIRE (9473)
http://www.wigjig.com
(for wire supplies and tools for crochet
and knitted jewelry)

Leather Craft Supplies
http://www.leather-crafts-supplies.com
(for large range of leather jewelry cords
and laces)

Shell Horizons, Inc.
14191 63rd Way
Clearwater, FL 33760
Tel: (727) 536-3333
http://www.seashellsonline.com
(for wholesale shells for jewelry)

Bella Beads
395 North State Street
Lake Oswego, OR 97035
Tel: (503) 635-2073
http://www.bellabeads-shop.com/
(for a selection of beads, semiprecious
stones, pearls, findings, and tools)

Elvee/Rosenberg
11 West 37th Street
New York, NY 10018-6235
Tel: (212) 575-0767
http://www.elveerosenberg.com/
(for a large collection of original vintage
glass beads)

Nordic Gypsy Beads and Jewelry
20 Third Street SW
Rochester, MN 55902
Tel: (507) 288-2258
http://www.nordicgypsy.com/
(for Japanese Delica, African, and
Czech beads)

Red Garnet Beads and Buttons
22002 64th Avenue W, Suite A
Mountlake Terrace, WA 98043
Tel: (425) 640-5441
http://www.red-garnet.com/
(for beads, new and vintage buttons,
tools, books, and classes)

Michael's: The Arts and Crafts Store
http://www.michaels.com
(for jewelry ideas and tips and general
bead supplies)

AC Moore
http://acmoore.com
(for special jewelry projects for kids and
online techniques)

Shipwreck Beads
8560 Commerce Place Dr. NE

Lacey, WA 98516
Tel: (360) 754-2323
http://www.shipwreck-beads.com
(for huge range of bead products from
different suppliers)

General Bead
Tel: (800) 545-6566
http://genbead.com/home2.htm
(for a catalogue of beads from
international suppliers)

Rio Grande
http://www.riogrande.com/index.asp
(for tools, equipment, and tips on
displaying your jewelry)

Back Room Beads
http://www.backroombeads.com
(for handmade lampwork beads made
from amber, glass, and gemstones)

Best Buy Beads
http://bestbuybeads.com
(for crystal, gold, and silver beads)

For a worldwide index to bead stores visit
this site:
http://www.guidetobeadwork.com/
localstores/index.htm#los

Index

Acknowledgments

Special thanks to Jan Eaton for making the gorgeous crocheted bead and wire necklace on page 74, Marie Clayton and Miranda Sessions at Collins & Brown for their attention to detail, and Lucinda Symons for the beautiful photography.

Many thanks also to Perivale-Gutermann Ltd for supplying beads, sequins, and thread.